Your Child Can't WEIGHT

Kimberly A. Hoffmann PharmD, BCPP

Jacqueline P. Hoffmann BA, MBA

Dedication

We dedicate this book to all the children who are struggling to control their surroundings and look to food as a solution.

About the Authors

Kimberly and Jacqueline Hoffmann are mother and daughter who currently reside in the southern valley of California. Both authors have had personal experiences dealing with childhood obesity. Kimberly is a single mother of five children and is also devoted to her parents, siblings, and friends with whom she loves to spend her free time. Dr. Hoffmann is a clinical professor of pharmacy practice and Regional Coordinator for the University of the Pacific in Stockton, California. In addition, Kimberly is a board certified psychiatric pharmacist who cares for patients with a variety of psychiatric diagnoses. Kimberly devotes time to her community by serving on boards and committees that deal with healthcare and psychiatry.

Jacqueline currently holds a bachelor's degree in communications and has recently graduated with a master's degree in business administration from the University of Saint Mary. While finishing her undergraduate degree, Jacqueline started a small trucking company that continues to expand. In addition, she is following her entrepreneurial aspirations of engaging in the fashion industry. These ventures are co-owned and operated by her loving partner, Eddie Arambula. Jacqueline is the oldest of five children and has always been family oriented. Over the years, she has developed a passion for fitness and self-improvement.

This book is a manifestation of Kimberly and Jacqueline's life experiences and their zeal for helping others with troublesome issues in their lives. The authors wrote this personal account with deep care and consideration for the children who are struggling by using food as a method to comfort themselves.

Table of Contents

Introduction

Americans have heard a great deal in the media about childhood obesity. Healthcare professionals are alarmed at the rapidly rising rate of children with diabetes, high blood pressure, and other serious health issues. These problems are related to obesity. The National Center of Health Statistics cites that in 2015, the prevalence of obesity was 8.9% among 2- to 5-year-olds compared with 17.5% of 6- to 11-year-olds, and 20.5% of 12- to 19-year-olds. Childhood obesity is also more common among certain populations.[1] When Michelle Obama was first lady of our country, she attempted to get involved in this rapidly accelerating issue. As a result, schools were mandated to serve healthier foods and ban foods thought to be less beneficial. This probably increased awareness in society about this serious issue, but the government's

---

[1] CDC/NCHS, National Health and Nutrition Examination Survey, 2011–2014.

involvement does not appear to have made any significant impact with this difficult social challenge. Although it is beneficial that our politicians and doctors recognize the problem, we believe that the true cause is not being addressed. The real cause is emotionally based. It is our wish to help parents in confronting and compassionately dealing with the emotional aspects of childhood obesity, resulting in happier and healthier children and adolescents who are struggling with this issue.

As a parent reading this book, you may feel we are solely blaming parents for this national epidemic. This is just not true. We realize that for you to be reading this book, you must love your child. You are putting in precious time to solve an issue that you may not know how to approach. When references are made throughout the book about children often having an issue with their weight as a response to a lack of love and/or attention, you may feel defensive. It is possible that you may think, *Who are these women? I love my child deeply, and s/he knows how much I love them. They have been showered with love and attention. If anything, maybe too much.*

We would like for every reader to know that we do not doubt that you love your child; however, the way a child may interpret your communication, may be very different than what you intended. Also, in this world where people are rushing around, and life has become frantic, it is difficult to give children the attention they truly need. So, in the time that you spend with your child, the interaction must be very meaningful. It may help for you to have a little background information about the two authors of this book.

(Kim)

I am first and foremost a single mother of five awesome children. From the age of eight, I was overweight. I will address this in more detail later in the book. I grew up in an upper middleclass family with two parents who are still happily married, and I was the middle child between two thin brothers. I am so fortunate to have a loving family and many wonderful friends and colleagues. I graduated from high school, and went on to college. Graduating with a Doctor of Pharmacy degree, I have worked in many areas of pharmacy. In 2002, I joined the faculty of my alma mater, the University of the Pacific, and am currently a Clinical Professor. In 2006, I became Board Certified in Psychiatry, and see patients in a psychiatric office. I have always been fascinated with human behavior and the study of the brain. I recognize that the true science of the mind, known as psychiatry, is closely linked with psychology. The two disciplines work most effectively together. This does not mean that children should all be placed on medications to combat this issue, but rather, that sometimes a psychiatric problem may exist, and first need to be addressed or ruled out as a cause for this problem. It is important that the reader understands that neither my daughter Jacqueline nor I, are licensed psychologists. We do believe that experts should be consulted if you feel your child is in emotional trouble or if there is any hint of suicidality. We are sharing our personal experiences and opinions in order to help the reader grasp the role that emotions often play in the development of childhood obesity. My oldest daughter, Jacqui, has also experienced and dealt with serious issues regarding her weight. We believe that communicating both of our perspectives will demonstrate that different family dynamics can play a significant role in the way that this problem is remedied. I continue to struggle with my weight issue, although I have progressed greatly. When habits are repeated for a long period of time, they become conditioned responses, and are more difficult to overcome. We will have paragraphs throughout the book that will be narratives of our personal experiences, which will be denoted by our first names.

(Jacqui)

I was also born into an upper middleclass family, living with two parents until the age of twelve. My father moved out of the house, my parents divorced, and I have had very little contact with my father since. My parents adopted three children who truly, in my heart, are my brothers and my sister. When I was seven years old, my parents also had another daughter who is my biologic sister. I am the oldest child in the family. I began to have issues with my weight at a very young age; however, after my father left our family, I felt much more comfortable about addressing my excess weight. I approached my mother for help, and she supported me. I began dieting and exercising at the age of 12, and had lost all of the excess weight within approximately one year. During high school, I went on some crazy, extreme diets that were not physically or mentally healthy. I now realize that I had not addressed the emotional reasons why I was eating. After graduating high school, I pursued a bachelor's degree in biochemistry with the intent of being like my mother, and becoming a pharmacist. Throughout my years in college, I struggled with choosing my career path, and ultimately believed communications was at the base of any future career that I chose. I changed my major to communications with a minor in psychology, and graduated in 2015. I have just finished my master's degree in business administration. In 2015, I also started a trucking company, and I am currently a co-owner of a clothing line. I am presently in a very healthy relationship with food and exercise, and am proud of the progress I have made with my mental and physical health. I believe it is important to highlight the parenting choices my mother made when raising an overweight daughter. I am hoping that parents who are reading this book will adopt these strategies and help their children to escape the conditioning that occurs when negative habits become lifelong coping mechanisms. I am excited to share my history and recovery from obesity with the desire to help anyone who is suffering from this condition.

Chapter 1

Your Child Can't Weight

(Kim)

As far back as I can remember, each night before falling asleep as a child, I would have one wish. I had watched shows where a genie would appear and grant the lucky recipient three wishes. The genie would say, "You can wish for anything that you desire except for three more wishes." I had my response all prepared: "I don't need three wishes, if you grant just this one, you can keep the other two. Please...please...help me to lose weight. I want to be thin." I think I always knew that genies were not real, but I went through this exercise night after night because I was desperate. It was all I could think about. I never did lose the weight, and I never did stop obsessing about this issue.

(Jacqui)

As a young child, I didn't wish to be thin until about 9-years old. As crazy as it sounds, I was very content with myself, and I did not obsess over my weight even though my dad started making hurtful comments to me regarding this issue. I remember I knew that I was the bigger girl in my class, but I never considered it a problem. Then, at age 9, I went to my friend's house and wondered why these two neighborhood girls said, "Who is that fat girl you're with?" I was shocked, and that is when it started. That was when I began looking at my body with disgust. Prior to this incident, I had attended a small Catholic school where I was sheltered from the usual harsh environment that overweight children often must endure. After three more years of snide and hurtful comments from my father about my weight, I had stored up a great deal of hurt and anger. My father had moved out of the house. I didn't want to lose the weight while my father was living with us, because I wanted to stand my ground and push against him. So, when he left, I began confronting my excess weight issue with my mom, and was successful in becoming thin.

It is difficult to be an overweight or underweight child, especially in America. We are all aware that the media and clothing designers fixate on creating the ideal thin body image. In their quest, there is a tendency for overweight individuals to feel rejected, and they often feel like they do not belong. We are certain that there are similar feelings for the children who are underweight, but because our experience has dealt with excess weight, the focus of this book will deal with the latter. These prejudices that society demonstrates against fat continue into adulthood, and excess weight causes emotional strife along with health problems for the individual. As a society, we like thin people, but we emphasize food in almost everything we do. Americans place food at the center of all celebrations and family gatherings. Birthday parties with globs of sugary frosting are the norm. Pizza parties are the easy and delicious endings to the schoolyear and at sporting events and any occasion where children or adolescents join together. Other common aspects of American life such as the heightened rate of divorce, families moving, and overly busy schedules, all may influence a child's tendency to seek food as comfort. In families where many members are obese, overeating is a way of life. When an individual in that family begins to lose weight or express their desire to, sabotage by the other members in the family or friends is more common than you may realize. The sabotage may manifest as lack of support or even direct acts that conflict with losing weight. An example of this would be a family member overtly pushing a plate of calorie-rich dessert to the person trying to develop healthy eating habits. In certain parts of the country, especially in the Midwest or in the South, feeding people is a way to show love.

(Kim)

I remember going to my grandmother's apartment for a family dinner. Grandma B was from Rockford, Illinois. This is the heart of the Midwest in America. Many women in the Midwest concentrate on serving men, and show their love for their families by laboring in the kitchen and serving big meals. My grandmother would sit on a kitchen stool next to the dinner table so that she could easily jump up to provide seconds on mashed potatoes and gravy or any other item that had been consumed. The family eating her dinner was the ultimate compliment for her. That meant her love was accepted and gave her value. This demonstration of love was carried on by my mother to her family.

(Jacqui)

A family friend was invited for Thanksgiving dinner. I was very focused on maintaining healthy eating habits throughout the holidays. I was following a rather strict eating program and wanted to achieve my goal of a lower body fat percentage. Instead of eating the food that the rest of the family consumed for Thanksgiving, I prepared grilled chicken and broccoli for my meal. I was careful not to announce what I was doing, because I did not want to draw attention away from the family event. As the food was served, our family friend couldn't help but vocally acknowledge my choice of food. She asked why I had to eat "special food" and said that she would never do the same thing. She then told me that what I was doing was ridiculous. I remember feeling anger and wondered why people have to focus on what other people put into their mouths.

(Kim)

My brothers and I were raised by the same parents, yet I was the only child with a weight problem. You might be thinking right now, "Then why were you the one with the weight problem?"

I believe I have always been a very sensitive person. I craved affection and wanted more focused attention from my mom than I received. My mother and grandmother were both very critical of my actions and behaviors.

My grandmother was very vocal about her preference for boys over girls. I remember her telling me that girls annoyed her with their giggling and silliness. Boys were put up onto a pedestal. She would harshly scold me for doing things that she would allow my brothers to do. She reminded me that I must always be ladylike. I realize now that she did the same thing to my mother. Despite the fact that my mom was the person who took care of my grandmother, she was treated as less than her brother because he was a man. I also remember my grandmother telling me that she would prefer to have twelve boys over having one girl. I believe that my grandma's hurtful thoughts and actions caused my mother to have a low sense of self-worth. My mom tried to change some of these learned behaviors when raising me; however, some of my grandmother's beliefs were transferred down.

Men and women often approach issues differently. The thought is that women are more sensitive about their bodies and personal issues. We disagree. Men and women are both sensitive regarding their self-images. Men often will not admit to this openly, especially in front of other men. This threatens their masculinity. But when you see a man who is obese, we believe the core of this problem is usually emotional. Some parents will often make more direct comments to a boy about their weight compared to a girl.

(Jacqui)

I witnessed a mother grabbing the extra fat around her son's midsection and she jokingly said, "What is this?" in front of other family members. Her intent was to bring awareness to her child about the existence of the extra weight in a harmless way, in an effort to motivate the child to eat healthier and exercise more. Parents, though, don't understand the impact they are making on their child's self-esteem. The parents don't think they are hurting their child's feelings, but remember, children are far more sensitive to comments than adults.

(Kim)

I have a family member who shared with me that her father nicknamed her the name of a dancing pig, Lulu, because she was overweight as a child. When she told me this story as an adult, she became emotionally upset and had to fight back tears. The father in this situation may have been attempting to communicate with his daughter in an endearing way or thought the comment was funny. What parents aren't recognizing is the tendency for children to internalize these remarks and attach them to their identity. The relative in the story above has had a lifelong struggle with food.

Women are thought to be more sensitive. Society, in general, is more careful when dealing with women and their weight. It is viewed as rude to ask a woman how much she weighs. We do not usually comment on what women eat, yet they will often eat less when they are around men. There is a thought that it is not feminine for women to consume a large amount of food.

(Kim)

I used to give parties for my female friends. We would eat and drink and I would have vendors at the house who would sell purses, jewelry, and other things that women loved to buy. I would order the same amount of food for that party as I would a party where the men would attend, because the women would barely eat when the men were invited. It astonished me how much food was consumed by the women when there were no men around.

While discussing ideas for this book with men, we often heard comments such as, "Oh that is such a load of crap. It comes down to calories in versus calories expended. That's it. You need to just get over all this emotional stuff and have some discipline." If that was the case, then why are we seeing obese professionals? Do you think that someone who is a CEO of a corporation who is 100 pounds overweight just doesn't have the intellect or strength to say no to food? These professionals have demonstrated great discipline in so many areas of their lives. They often work long hours when others are too tired to do so. They recognize problems in organizations and strategically plan how to solve these issues, yet it is thought that people who are obese are intellectually weak and are often the butt of jokes and disrespect. How many intelligent people do you know who are overweight and experiencing a serious health related issue such as diabetes or heart disease? If they are truly intelligent, why aren't they more disciplined? Once again, these individuals seem to have plenty of discipline regarding other areas of their lives. They hold down impressive jobs, pay their bills, raise their children, and help others in society. Yet, they seem to struggle with this very important issue.

Many people are not aware of why they struggle. They do not see the impact that family traditions have on their own actions. The experiences that families go through may affect or be perceived by one individual differently than by other family members. Childhood disappointments often play a significant role in how people conduct themselves as adults. These childhood hurts are often hidden or suppressed because human beings try to avoid pain. People often will develop unhealthy eating habits as methods of coping with negative experiences.

Chapter 2

Trauma is a Loaded Word

According to Webster's Dictionary, trauma is "a very difficult or unpleasant experience that causes someone to have mental or emotional problems usually for a long time." Trauma is a loaded word. In society today, trauma has been molded into meaning a horrific and unusual experience that renders a person incapable of living normally. We associate trauma with gruesome stories of torture, people witnessing murder, and sexual perversions. In this book, we want to desensitize the word and to recognize that trauma does not have to be associated with anything disgusting or prohibitive. Childhood trauma places an indelible imprint on your life, and plays a part in the decisions you make as an adult. This is why it is so important that we help children through difficulties before they incorporate these experiences into established habits. Children do not understand how to process trauma. Often they bury or suppress the pain. This pain eventually surfaces and manifests itself as acting out, substance abuse, depression that may result in extreme isolation, anxiety, or in many other ways. It is not uncommon for these trauma victims to mimic the behaviors of those who did the initial abusing. For example, we may hear of a man who saw his mother abused physically, and then may also abuse his wife. Sexual abuse also often extends through many generations.

When most individuals hear the term "abuse" they often immediately think of rape, physical beatings, and other gruesome acts, but actions that may seem less serious to some people are interpreted as traumatic to the person experiencing them.

When a child is sexually or physically abused, they perceive themselves as someone who is not worthy. If someone abuses them, they must not be worth much. This becomes the mantra the child lives her/his life upon. Lowered self-esteem is the direct result. We tend to believe that women are sexually molested far more than men. No one is sure what the exact statistics are for either gender, because sexual trauma is often hidden and not spoken about.

(Kim)

Probably the most surprising aspect of sexual abuse that I discovered with my patients was how many males are sexually molested as children by other men. In certain cultures, it is much more prevalent. Men will recall these experiences and are often ashamed. They will admit that the sexual experience may have felt good physically and because of that, they question their sexuality. They will scold themselves and have even told me they should have done something more to stop it. They will become tearful and admit to me that they have shared this information with no one else. They know I am bound by confidentiality and that allows them to seek help through me. These men will often overeat, drink excessively, or even take drugs in an effort to numb the pain of the abuse. Intimacy becomes difficult in most of their relationships as a result of the trauma.

Perhaps the most damaging emotion a human being may have is shame. Shame evokes a feeling in the victim of being a bad person. It results in people being very sensitive to judgement by others. These people will imagine that their actions are being scrutinized and judged by everyone. In the context of overeating, people who were shamed as a child often hide their eating, or eat while alone to avoid comments or criticisms from others. These behaviors may also lead to a person isolating her/himself from others. When human beings do not interact socially, often depression worsens. It is important to separate an unwanted behavior on the part of a child from the child's identity. Parents or authority figures have so much power over the way a child views her/himself. As we age, we usually become less sensitive to comments from others, but children magnify the smallest comments made by the people they love. Parents usually hold the most significant power in this arena. Parents are a child's primary role models. If a child is told s/he is weak, s/he will most often live up to this characterization; or in contrast, may vow to do everything in their power to be the opposite. This may explain why we see families where one or two of the children rise above the extreme dysfunction of the others.

(Kim)

I remember many stories from my childhood that center around my weight issue. I was extremely sensitive about my problem and lived in fear that people would embarrass me with their comments, their looks, or their teasing. My mother was very upset that I did not look like my friends. I clearly remember one Sunday evening meal where my mother had served a pot roast, potatoes, vegetables, and dinner rolls. About halfway through the dinner, I had eaten my roll and really wanted a second one. I reached over and started to grab another roll. I felt my mother's glare from the end of the table. Her eyes were staring at me, her lips were taunt, and I dropped the bread back into the basket. I felt she was angry and I knew I was disappointing her again. Later that evening, I quietly took a roll out of the kitchen and ran back to my room where I ate it behind my locked bedroom door. I felt ashamed like I was doing something wrong, but I felt that the food helped fill a place of emptiness inside me. This became a habit throughout my life and to this day, I struggle to replace this emptiness with something healthier than excess food.

Another way parents may affect their children without realizing it is by not giving them enough attention. The fast pace we are all living in today can be exhausting. Many parents are both working to try to make ends meet and to provide for their families. There seems to be a pursuit for more toys and material objects in an effort to show love and to entertain children. This electronic age where people are watching television, playing video games, and playing on their tablets has led to a more solitary lifestyle for everyone. Human beings are social animals, and face-to-face interaction has dramatically declined as a result of this technological era. It is interesting that while this form of entertainment has attained popularity, we keep hearing that the numbers of people suffering from depression in America has also skyrocketed. The media seems to have become a more significant influence in our children's lives. A lack of parental attention may be experienced by a child as an emptiness or loneliness, and may be perceived as pain or discomfort. Substance abuse is also often a way that human beings avoid pain or discomfort. Food is usually the substance that is most accessible to children as they do not generally have money or transportation to obtain other substances such as drugs or alcohol. This technological era also means less physical movement on behalf of many people. We keep hearing about sedentary lifestyles that lead to obesity and poor health outcomes. It seems our children are less healthy than at any other time in the history of America. When we aren't paying attention to our children, we are losing a window of time to educate them about life. Children are often left to try to figure things out on their own.

With the barrage of information coming at them through television and other forms of media, they must decide for themselves what is appropriate and what is not. This may be very stressful for children and leave them floundering for answers. Food may become a way to self-soothe when the child is upset. The warmth or weight of the food in the stomach may resemble the warmth of parental love to some children.

(Kim)

When I was a child, my mother would take my brothers out to practice baseball in a little league. I would be left at home to watch television and this is where I developed the worst of my eating habits. I loved being home alone without my mother there, because then I would fill up on Twinkies, ice cream, or anything else that I was not allowed to consume in her presence. This made me feel content and full. It seemed to replace the feelings of warmth and of love that I so craved.

(Jacqui)

I remember wanting to eat ice cream or macaroni and cheese. These two foods provided comfort to me. I knew that my father would not approve of me eating these types of foods because they would worsen my weight problem. I was scared of the consequences of him finding out that I had eaten outside of mealtime. I began to sneak these foods and learned how to get around his watchful eye. The house we lived in had wooden floors that would make sounds when people walked on them. I could determine who was walking around based on the sounds of their footsteps. I mastered the sound of my father's footsteps and would listen closely as they disappeared down the hallway so that I could sneak the foods I loved.

Many parents believe in restricting their children from certain foods to prohibit them from gaining weight. They label these foods as "bad," and scold them when that food is consumed. It is important for you to understand that your child is smarter than you may realize and s/he will probably find a way to eat those foods if it is important to them. The corrective action that is often much more successful in this situation is to allow them to have the food, without harsh connotation, and this is a good time to observe your child's moods and behaviors. You may consistently ask them how they are feeling before and after they have eaten the food. It may help you to identify if the child is using food to mask feelings or unwanted emotions. This helps your child to become aware of how her/his body is feeling. For example, if your child eats a big slice of cake and then complains that her/his stomach hurts, you may want to make the following remark: "When I eat heavy sugary sweets it often causes my stomach to hurt also, and I don't like the way my body feels after I have eaten a lot of sugar." Then, leave it there, unless your child asks you a question. Your child has heard what you have said. S/he will think about this long after the discussion is over.

Chapter 3

Kim's Feelings as an Overweight Child

(Kim)

Well, here I am in front of the computer. I have been trying to figure out what to say in this chapter. It is not because there is a lack of material to write about, but rather it is a subject of great vulnerability for me. How much of my secret do I want to expose? Is it a secret? The entire world can see that I am very overweight. Why would anyone choose to be so overweight? "Just stop eating so much." How many times have I heard that? The Hoffmann family is a prideful bunch. Most of us would rather keep our private lives to ourselves. To sit down and write this personal account is very difficult for me and rather embarrassing, which says to me that I must write it. The only true way to rid yourself of something you fear is to tackle it head on. I do not wish to hurt anyone with my story, but feel that I must be open and honest in order to achieve my ultimate goal of helping people who are dealing with similar weight issues.

This chapter, and the two chapters that come after it written by my daughter and my parents, are probably the most important for the parents of overweight children to read. They are open and honest accounts of what it feels like to be a child who is screaming for help or a concerned frustrated parent who wants to help her/his child. I see children often in my psychiatric private practice who are usually brought to the office for reasons other than their weight issues.Usually, they are in my office because the child is acting out in some other manner. They have failing grades in school, they aren't getting along with their siblings or other children, etc. I have found that these kids don't have a lot to say while their parents are in the room. As soon as I have the parents step out of the office, I often get a waterfall of tears and a lot of sadness pouring out of these children. You may be thinking, "Wow,

I'm glad my children feel safe enough to share their feelings with me." Or you may be thinking that these parents must be awfully harsh and oppressive to the children when they are at home. For the most part, I find that the children do not want to hurt their parents' feelings. They are protecting their parents by not saying how they really feel. I find this happens a great deal in families where there has been a separation or a divorce. Often the child is mourning the loss of closeness between her/himself and either or both of the parents. One child told me, "My mother's new boyfriend is getting in the way of the time my mom and I spend together. She always wants to be with him, and when she isn't with him, she is usually on the phone with him."

But what about those children who are in families where their parents are still married? I see there is still a feeling of loss by the child of a relationship with one or both of the parents. The parents may be there trying to "get it all done" in this crazy busy life we are living. These parents are working so hard to make a good life for their children, yet their children feel they are not there for them. The loss is not about the amount of time, it is rather the closeness or lack of closeness felt by the child to the parent. We think of intimacy in the context of a man and a woman, or in a romantic love relationship, but I believe relationships between parents and their children should be very intimate.

That is what is usually missing; the emotional connection between a parent and her/his child. It may be there with one parent, but not the other. It may be missing with both parents. If a child feels a void in this relationship that they emotionally yearn for, the child will often put something else in place of that to comfort themselves. It may be food, it may be drugs or alcohol, an emotional wall, sexual acts, or any other way that self-soothes them. You can see these behaviors are often passed down through many generations.

At this point, I need to say that there are other reasons that a child may be eating inordinate amounts of food.

One possibility could be that the child may be experiencing physical or sexual abuse. I once had a psychologist tell me that 85 percent of all females with an obesity issue have been sexually molested. The thought is that since being overweight is such an unattractive attribute in American society, the act of keeping yourself fat will cause members of the opposite sex to not be attracted to you and will leave you alone sexually. I certainly see this in adults that were molested as children, along with intense anxiety, depression, and the inability to be intimate with anyone. So, what about those of us who were not sexually molested? I believe that if there was a history of any type of abuse, the child often experiences the loss of intimacy we spoke of above. Abuse may occur as sexual abuse, physical violence, emotional berating, or by ignoring or neglecting the child. Human beings need physical and emotional connections to other people in order to feel fulfilled. This begins with the relationship with their parents. It is usually where we develop our sense of self-esteem. When there is dysfunction in one of our parental relationships, and it is not addressed, the child will often attempt to find a way to make the situation bearable.

The term self-esteem is bandied about a great deal. I remember watching a television program and hearing Oprah Winfrey say that she believed that at the root of most emotional problems was low self-esteem. I believe she is correct. When a child is abused verbally, sexually, physically beaten, or ignored, a message is being sent to that child that s/he is not to be valued.

They are not good enough. To be ignored as a child, translates to that child that what s/he says or feels does not matter. They are not important. When I went to a psychologist after my divorce, he stressed to me how important this concept is to a child. I was concerned about my children and how the divorce and separation from their father was impacting their behavior. The psychologist that I consulted regarding parenting told me to talk to my children, and if they made a statement to me that I did not know how to answer, then I should repeat back what they said to me. For example, if my son said, "I am so mad at my dad right now, why doesn't he show up to see me?" I might say back to him, "I understand that you are very angry right now with your dad, it feels awful that he didn't show up to see you today." I said nothing new to him about a situation that I could not control, but my son knew that I was listening to him, and that what he had to say was important. This advice was fabulous. It helped me in so many situations that I was not sure how to handle. I see how vital it is to nurture a child with regard to self-esteem. I am not advocating handing out trophies to children for just showing up, but rather engaging with a child to help him/her embrace their sense of self-

worth. If a child repeatedly does not feel that her/his feelings or actions are recognized, they often carry this desire for attention and validation into their adult life.

So back to my personal journey.

I remember my childhood as being consumed in feelings of shame. I knew I was not like the other kids, and I desperately wanted to lose weight. I have a vivid memory of lying in bed one evening and telling my mother how much I wanted to be thin. I also remember my weight issue as the big problem that no one in my family dared to speak about except my mother. It felt so shameful and disgusting to be overweight and no one wanted to bring it up. The first time I felt different from the other children with regard to my weight was in third grade. I remember that one of the girls in class would give me her potato chips from her lunch every day. My mother always packed an apple with my sandwich, and it just wasn't as satisfying to me. So wanting the high-calorie carbohydrates started very early for me. I began gaining a great deal of weight, and my mother was very upset over it. I am certain that my mother wanted the best for me, but she was always very unhappy with my extra weight. I remember many situations where my mother spoke with me regarding my problem. I have added a few of these memories into this book to help parents understand how their attempts at solving this problem may not be helpful to their child.

One day my mother decided to take me to buy a new dress for a special occasion. She even took me to "Louella's Boutique", which was a higher-end children's clothing store. We chose a couple of dresses, and headed for the dressing room. My mom was in the room with me, and as I tried on the first dress, it was too tight. I remember looking up at my mom's face, and she looked extremely angry. She didn't say anything to me, but it was obvious that she was not happy. I tried on the second dress, and it was too small also. I felt so horrible. My mother grabbed the dress from me, and raising her voice she said, "Kimberly, I can't believe this. I told myself I wasn't going to say anything, but you can't fit into anything. You have gained so much weight, that nothing in this store fits you."

I knew the other people in the store could hear the entire conversation, and I was embarrassed and humiliated. All I wanted to do was to run out of the store. I felt so ashamed. It was so important to me to please my mother, and I always had a very hard time doing that.

Another memory is one that also occurred in third grade. My mother was driving me home from school. This was really special in my mind, because we usually went back and forth to school in a carpool with my brothers and other neighborhood children who attended the same Catholic school. I remember thinking, "I get to sit up in the front seat with Mom, it is just she and I." We began talking about my day, and I asked her what kind of school she went *to when she was a little girl. Looking back on the situation, I'm sure I must have struck a sensitive chord with her or something, because she looked over at me raising her voice and said, "Why do you always ask such stupid questions?" She continued on a rant yelling at me, and I remember sliding down on the seat thinking, "Please stop yelling at me."*

These exchanges were excruciating to me. I yearned to be close to my mom. It was apparent to me that my extra weight or something else about me embarrassed or disgusted her. I now believe she felt responsible for my weight problem. On one occasion, she told me she used to be overweight as a child. She even told me a story where my grandmother would bring home clothes in the largest size, and have to let them out at the seams to fit my mother. When I asked my mom how she lost the weight, she told me, as she grew, the weight just came off. I was so happy to hear this.

I was hoping the same thing would happen for me. It was obvious to me that being overweight was something to be ashamed of. From then on, my mom was determined to get me to lose weight. She took me to Weight Watchers™, offered me one dollar for every pound I lost, and she told me the cherry pies, ice cream, and Twinkies were off limits for me. Only my brothers were to eat them and I was to eat fruit and vegetables for snacks. This is when I started sneaking food. I was always afraid of the judgement that would happen when people saw what I was eating. I have this issue even today.

Another reason I believe I may have kept eating the food that I was told to stay away from was an attempt at gaining power or control over my life and my decisions. For me, I was angry inside, but did not realize the emotion was anger. I was wanting to be accepted and loved for who I was and I never seemed to be good enough. As I have gotten older, I realized that my mom was not trying to hurt me. My mother had many unresolved issues from her childhood regarding her sense of self-worth. She chose to seek her value as a person through her husband and her children. As a result, I was never able to satisfy this need for my mother.

Third grade was a traumatic year for me. It was also the year that I was publicly humiliated in front of my class at school. We were going to be dressing up as elves in the school Christmas play.

A mother of one of my classmates was sewing the costumes. We were to wear a leotard under the elf costume. The daughter of the seamstress, Roseanne, who was a classmate, walked in and very loudly announced that there were two leotards missing from the bag. She said, "My mom has to special order the leotards for Kim and Kathy because they need to be in bigger sizes." She then started laughing. I was mortified. One of the boys in my class, Gerald, started laughing and pointing at me. This made me begin to avoid taking part in any situation or activity that could possibly result in embarrassment due to my weight.

I grew up in Bakersfield, California, where the summers are very hot. Just about everyone I knew lived in a house with a swimming pool. It became a problem to swim anywhere other than my pool or in my best friend's pool. All of the other girls wore two-piece bathing suits, and I wore a one piece that covered my stomach. It is hard to be a kid, and to be different. My friends were very nice to me and didn't mention "my problem."

One day I went swimming at one of my friend's houses. Her sister went inside and got my pants, and put them on. She came outside by the pool wearing them. She was not only a thin girl, she was also a couple of years younger than I was, so the pants looked very large on her. She said, "Look everybody, I'm Kim Hoffmann!" She laughed and laughed. I felt paralyzed. I didn't know what to do. I then eventually got out of the pool, put my clothes on, and made up a false excuse explaining why I had to go home.

This was another incident that enhanced my propensity to isolate myself from any possible embarrassing situations. I made up reasons why I could not attend swimming parties, I worried about never having to be publicly weighed, and I would dread having to go to the doctor for any reason in fear of being weighed. I have missed out on so many fun times throughout my life because of this fear. Because I could not compete with my friends when it came to boys, I found other ways to obtain positive recognition.

Right after third grade, I began to excel in school. My grades were always very good. I decided to start the first yearbook that my junior high ever had. I was the editor. I became involved in student government and anything else where my body was not an issue. It became important to me to be good at something. I attributed so many of my failures to my weight. In junior high, I lost the election to be secretary by three votes. I convinced myself it was because I was not thin. I'm sure that I attributed losses to my weight that had nothing to do with the size of my body.

I always had a large number of friends. These were both guys and girls. People often commented on the fact that they thought I was such a nice girl. I was careful to please people, because I knew if I didn't, they might call me fat or draw attention to my one very shameful quality. I also continued to be nice to keep people from yelling at me like my mother often did. I felt that I had this one big flaw that everyone could see. I continued to eat privately to fill the empty place inside. I realize now that the emptiness is in my heart, not my stomach. Because I have self-soothed this way all of my life, it has become a conditioned response. It is a habit. I become upset if I think I cannot eat if I want to. It is a control issue that I am sure stems back to the hard glaring stares across the table from my mother when I went to get a second helping of food.

My father chose to deal with the problem quietly. He always let me know he loved me. On one occasion I overheard my mother telling my father that he had to say something to me to get me to lose weight. He asked her what she wanted him to say, and she told him that he needed to tell me to cut this out because I am too fat, and that I had better get the weight off. An hour later or so, I came out of my room and my father said, "Kimberly, you are too heavy, you need to stop eating so much, and I mean it."

When he said this to me I felt a lump in my throat and my body felt frozen. I managed to murmur a soft "OK" because I didn't know how else to respond. I just wanted to get out of the room as quickly as possible. It would've been so much better if he or my mother would have sat me down and asked me about my feelings regarding food and why I was eating. They could have let me know their love for me had nothing to do with the size of my body. I felt I had no one to talk to regarding this issue.

When I finished my junior year in high-school, my mother came in and told me she had found a weight loss camp in Washington state to send me to for seven weeks. She had me booked on the airplane and I was going in two days. She never asked me about how I felt about going and it was going to be the first time I travelled anywhere without my family or an adult accompanying me. I was scared, but as usual I did what I was told. I worked very hard while I was there exercising and eating very little. I called home every week and the first question from my mom was, "How much weight did you lose this week?"

I remember wishing that she would just once ask me how I was feeling. I lost thirty-two pounds in seven weeks. I dreaded going home because I still was not thin. I looked much better, but I still had some weight to lose. As I arrived home, I saw my family waiting for me, and my mom's face dropped. She was obviously disappointed with my results.

I then went out for the varsity volleyball team at school. I worked out doing double sessions, and I made it through each cut until the last one. I was the last girl cut from the team. I was so disappointed and ashamed. When my mom picked me up from practice, I did not tell her. I had been crying, and I didn't want to see her disappointment. From that time on, I stopped exercising and dieting in high school. I felt I had failed. As I had been slowly isolating myself from activities, my enjoyment in life was redirected toward food.

This problem became all-encompassing in my life and it is still a subject that is always at the forefront of my thoughts. I believe many of the choices I made at that time, and later in life regarding men, were poor choices as a result of my low self-esteem. I felt I was lucky to have men interested in me because I felt I was horribly unattractive physically due to the weight.. I have had difficulty in the past separating my intellectual or professional self from my emotional being. I have always believed in my intellectual abilities, and I have exceled in this way. Emotionally, I have struggled to feel that I am worthy of attention and love. I seem to attract men who have difficulties in intimacy or an ability to be close. At the age of twenty-three, I underwent gastric bypass surgery. This procedure was very new at the time, and my surgeon made a mistake while cutting above my stomach. He left a portion of the intestine too short, and I had many problems.

I lost a great deal of weight, but still never made it to my goal. I had many problems with this surgery because I had not addressed the true emotional issues for my eating. I also had many years of throwing up and chronic, severe anemia. In 2007, my gastric bypass was reversed. I had a surgeon who attempted a very difficult repair. I developed several infections and had a trying few years rebounding from many hospitalizations. I have gotten through the physical issues with my stomach, and due to my *surgeon, my stomach has now fully healed. I continue to struggle with the emotional aspects of my eating, and as a result, have gained the weight I had previously lost back again.*

Chapter 4

Jacqui's Feelings as an Overweight Child

(Jacqui)

I have avoided writing this chapter every time I've had the opportunity to do so. Thinking about revisiting the place, the mentality and emotions that I've worked so hard to transform, is a very scary idea. When I want something in this world I go after it without hesitation, but going back to this vulnerable territory doesn't seem to evoke the same enthusiasm as usual. Although I have a very assertive, confident personality in most aspects of my life, there are still tender subjects and hidden scars that I believe will never fully heal. Just sitting here, at twenty-three years old and reflecting on how much I've changed with regard to my perspective of weight in the last ten years is what gives me the courage to share my experiences with you.

To be honest, I can't remember a time when I wasn't overweight during my childhood. I remember seeing a picture from preschool and thinking, "Ok, see, I wasn't always overweight as a child," but actually remembering being young and thin is not something I can recall. During grade school, I became a very friendly student that was helpful to others around me and fervently tried to seek approval from peers and authority figures through good behavior and compassion. I wanted to embody the perfect child.

I even remember my best friend's mom in second grade telling me she wished I was her child because I was so well behaved. I absorbed this comment like a sponge because it made me feel worthy and valuable as a human being. More than anything, the one person I wanted to please was my father and somehow, at six-years old, I always came up short.

"You're going to sit at this table and finish every last bit of food on your plate, Paige." (As a child I was called by my middle name,

Paige.) I still remember his index finger two feet from my face as he stood glaring down at me from across the kitchen table. All of my brothers and sisters had been excused from the table but I still had a pile of grapes on my plate. You must understand, the thought of swallowing a raw grape made me physically want to vomit unlike any other food. I didn't understand why everyone else was allowed to not finish their food but I had to sit in agony. I remember thinking, "It's all right, I can sit here and he will eventually let me leave the table." Nope. I sat there while everyone else bustled around the kitchen cleaning dishes, putting food away, and hurrying off to their rooms. He looked at me and told me again, "You're going to sit at this table and finish every last bit of food on your plate, Paige." I had held my ground for so long, I couldn't give up now. But then he reminded me of his power with those domineering eyes and I cowered down. He forced me to eat those damn grapes, and I remember feeling so enraged at him unlike any other emotion I had ever felt. This was not typical for the sweet, well-mannered kid I felt I was.

The "grape incident" is the first time I remember loathing my own father. Edward T. Smith III was a US Marine for several years and adopted the power-hungry tactics used in the military to raise his own children. My father made sure we all knew he was the authority figure in the house and he held the ultimate power. His thirst for control is the force that made me eat that grape, to show his six-year old his ability to make her crumble. Little did he know, these small instances ignited a strong burning desire in me for the same power he tried to take away from me.

Being a Brownie Girl Scout in the third grade was such a fun part of being a kid. I was friends with most of the girls and really enjoyed spending our Wednesday afternoons doing arts and crafts and learning about our role in the community. At this point in my childhood, I was easily thirty pounds overweight, but I had attended a private Catholic school and the environment mixed with my friendly personality prevented the bullying and teasing that you hear many overweight children often suffer. Many of my classmates liked me and I believe didn't want to hurt my feelings because I was so sweet. During the year, the scout mom organized a trip for the scouts to go to a store called "Limited Too" for a fashion party. Limited Too was like Nordstrom for a young girl: Heaven.

All the mothers accompanied their daughters for the big Girl Scout event. I remember being so excited to do a fashion show at the store. I could barely contain myself. On the drive over, I do remember thinking, "I wonder if they will have clothes in my size," but it was like my mom read my mind as she verbally assured me we would have fun and be able to find plenty of things to wear. That was my mom, always making sure I knew everything would be okay. As we entered the store, all the girls started shopping, *finding multiple pieces of clothing to wear and heading for the fitting rooms. As I started to realize not many items would fit, I became frantic about finding one thing to fit my body. Again, my mom maintained a very calm, happy attitude as she looked at me and told me we'd find something. This was the first time I truly felt different and less attractive than the other girls, despite my mother's genuine effort to make me feel better.*

As I noticed the differences between me and the other girls, aesthetically, I began idolizing thin, pretty women. I remember looking at the young girls that modeled for children's advertisements and the women in magazines and yearning to look like them more than anything. I tried to envision what it would be like to be a thin person and be able to fit into all the clothes in the store. I craved to be beautiful. Starting to realize I couldn't magically change my physical body into the models I saw, which caused me to feel unworthy and unsatisfied, I began to turn to food as my source of fulfillment to block these negative feelings.

All I knew was no matter how badly I felt, ice cream always made me feel better. The texture, the cold creamy sensation of just about any flavor of ice cream temporarily took away the pain. When I finished a bowl, I remember wanting to have that feeling again, even if my stomach was full, just to feel good. My father would only allow me to have a little bit of ice cream and scold me about having too much because "ice cream was bad". My constant desire for feeling good resulted in me sneaking the ice cream into my room whenever he was asleep so I could go to my happy place without punishment or judgement for eating "badly".

On top of telling me what I could and could not eat, my father often ridiculed my siblings and me over just about any issue. One day, he decided that I would help him tear down the backyard *fountain with a jackhammer. He thought the physical work would provide exercise for me and it would force me to lose some weight.*

"Paige! Get out here. Help your brother and I get rid of these rocks!" I still remember his extremely loud, overbearing, militant voice through the echoes of the hallway startling me. If I didn't get up and do what he said then I would really get it. It had to have been over 100 degrees in Bakersfield that day as I went outside in my tennis shoes and my father handed me a pair of gloves to put on. He told me I needed to pick up all the rocks that fell on the ground as he used a jackhammer to destroy a built-in fountain from the ground. As I started to pick up the rocks he would turn the machine off every couple of minutes and tell me, "Move faster!" or "Come on, hurry up!" "Start sweating! Move! Move! Move!"

I remember wanting to punch him in the face. I was tired, miserably hot, and started pleading with him to please let me go inside. If this was exercise, I never wanted to do it again in my life.

Nothing I did outside with my father and brother that day was ever right. I didn't work hard enough. I didn't move fast enough. I was, again, a disappointment.

I associated exercise with pain and struggling at this point in my life. I then found out in fourth grade that my physical education class would require children to perform standardized tests of strength and health around the country. As if I hadn't formed a negative-enough attitude toward exercise, now I was going to be forced to do something I feared. There was one specific incident that scared me more than anything...

Everyone in the fourth grade was going to have to run the mile. I knew I couldn't run the whole thing, but I was going to try my best because I didn't want to be last again. Our teacher, Mr. Abbott, led us out to the track and told us what time we would have to meet to qualify for a passing grade. Knowing there was no way I would score a passing grade on this activity, my only desire was to finish the mile run without being last or giving up. I began to run and started to see everyone slowly passing me, one by one on the track. On my third lap, I was tired; I could barely move my feet. The excess weight on my body started to make me feel like I was going to faint. I began to feel this sharp pain in my side and I thought I was going to die. At the end of the third lap, I was barely able to talk as I was gasping for air. I told Mr. Abbott I couldn't finish the run because I couldn't breathe. Tears began to fall from my eyes. I felt like such a disappointment.

Mr. Abbott was a very young, athletic man and I feared his negative judgment about my inability to complete the activity. As I closed my eyes waiting for him to tell me something negative about my weight, he looked at me and said, "Ok sweetie come with me." Mr. Abbott handed his stopwatch to the other student that wasn't able to run the mile because of an ankle injury from her club soccer tournament, and he escorted me to the water fountain. Not once did this man say anything about my weight or not being able to finish. Instead, he took a compassionate stance and told me everything would be ok. Feeling relieved about not upsetting my teacher, I began to relax and told him thank you.

To this day, I've wanted to find Mr. Abbott and thank him for just accepting me the way I was as a child and tell him the impact he has had on my life. There are many parental or authority figures that believe it is their job to tell a child what s/he is doing wrong and what they need to do to change. Mr. Abbott knew I knew the reason why I couldn't finish the race. There was no need to rub the excess pounds in my face and make me feel ashamed of my body. For someone who was extremely fit and seemed health conscious, I didn't expect this compassionate, loving behavior, yet I soaked it up and remember thanking God that I didn't disappoint another male role model.

Another reason I chose to be a "people pleaser" throughout elementary school was to prevent other kids from making fun of me and it worked. During first through third grades, kids are generally sweet and mirror the attitude you give them, but as children get older this genuine innocence begins to disappear. Starting to realize the magnitude of my weight gain, I wanted to avoid any chance of being mocked or bullied by other kids because I knew my weight problem was an easy target. I decided to try out for drama at school, and ended up loving to act. Despite my growing insecurity, I had no problem getting up in front of a large audience and projecting my voice as I enacted the personality of another individual. I loved it until I started to notice the trend of my roles. In the play Oliver Twist, I was chosen to play the role of Mrs. Mann. In another play about the greatest jazz legends, I played the role of Ella Fitzgerald. A common theme started to emerge: I played the heavier-set women. The idea of being an overweight person was becoming a way of life. It wasn't until I played the role of a woman who wasn't overweight that I realized I couldn't hide my insecurity.

The lights were all turned off. The whispers of the excited children flooded backstage as the parents patiently waited for the performance. The teachers were constantly placing their index fingers over their mouths in an attempt to quiet the noises from the cast. I remember feeling confident behind the curtain, proudly waiting for the show to begin.

As everyone was getting into position, I overheard an older boy tell his friend, "Hey, look, the girl in the red dress on stage looks like she's pregnant!" The giggles the two boys shared made me mad because I knew how desperately the teachers were trying to get everyone to be quiet, not realizing they were referring to me. As I began to let go of my anger I started to look around, I noticed I was the only girl wearing a red dress on center stage. My heart dropped as reality started to sink in. Despite my feelings of embarrassment, I knew I had an obligation to play my role and I couldn't stand the thought of letting down the people that were counting on me. I gave an outstanding performance.

As I got older, I wasn't quite as extroverted and outgoing as I was when I was younger. I began feeling extremely self-conscious about my body and opting out of attending outdoor activities like pool parties to prevent further embarrassment. One year, my aunt and uncle invited me to go on a trip with my extended family to Hawaii when I was in seventh grade and I could hardly contain my excitement. I had so much fun on that vacation and had so many experiences I will never forget. When we were all on our way home, I realized how excited I was to see my family, especially my mom.

After unpacking my luggage, I decided to go into my mom and dad's room to talk to my mom about the trip. I could spend hours *with my mom without noticing it. I loved being with her. As I grew sleepy I could hear my father's footsteps coming down the hallway and knew it was time to go to bed.*

As I started to get up, my dad came into the room with a smile on his face and said, "Come on, it's time for bed you fat lard!" Seeing the smile on his face I couldn't tell whether to force myself to laugh with him and make it a joke, or burst into tears. I knew my father thought I was overweight, but never did I feel so unloved and ugly as I did in that moment. Hearing the comment, my mother came unglued and told my father how uncalled for and horrible his remark was. Not wanting to be the reason for my father's anger at the rejection of this joke, I ran to my room and cried uncontrollably into my pillow.

To top off this experience, I would go over to my friend's house and other girls started making quiet comments about my weight.

One time I went to my friend's house, and she decided to introduce me to her neighborhood girls.

My friend at the time was extremely thin and petite. When we went outside to put our helmets on and ride down to meet her friends, a group of girls came walking across the driveway. The house was on a deep slope and we stopped to look down at them at the bottom of the hill. We could hear what the girls were saying, I heard one of them say, "Who's the fat girl though?" Their giggles triggered the memory of the two boys mocking my weight in drama. As I began to feel a rush of embarrassment and hurt, my friend shot a look directly at me to see my reaction.

Not wanting to cause a problem or make a scene, I quickly forced the tears down my throat and asked my friend if she knew who the girls were. She looked down and mumbled, "Those are the friends we were going to meet."

Besides the differences other individuals were pointing out between my body and those of other kids, I began trying to prevent situations that would draw attention to me. I constantly feared the kids would take the bigger size PE belts for flag football and I wouldn't have one that fit. I avoided end-of-the-year parties that would require me to wear a swimsuit; I chose not to participate in any sports because I feared rejection. I also started to greatly fear males. All of these situations started to pile up just as quickly as the excess pounds did around my waist.

During the end of my seventh-grade year in school, my father decided to leave our family in the middle of the night and I have chosen to have little contact with him since. I remember driving home with my mother one evening and telling her I wanted to lose weight. Never before had I expressed my desire to lose weight to my mother or father and I truly believe my father's departure was the action that allowed me to ask for help. I still remember my mother looking at me in the car with a warm, endearing smile and she said, "Ok, honey, how can I help you?" I told my mom I wanted to go to Jenny Craig and start to learn how to eat healthfully. I wanted to exercise after I finished my homework in the evening, but I was too young to go to the gym, and it was dark outside at that time. My mother bought a treadmill for the family, and I asked her if I could put it in my room. She allowed the man to assemble the equipment in my room. For my entire eighth-grade year, I ate healthfully and ran on that treadmill until I lost the weight. I remember having conversations with my friend, who was also overweight, and I started telling her how I envisioned a finish line where all the thin people were on one side and I could see myself crossing that line into a new, healthier body. I replayed that image so often in my head that it felt real. I would put my headphones on and take out my anger, frustration, and resentment towards my father on the treadmill. Music became the channel I could release my emotions through, and my treadmill helped the tension and pain leave my heart.

Looking back, as my father was looking at me eating those grapes, I vowed in my head that I would find a way to maintain my own power. My father tried to control what I put in my mouth, and I retaliated by sneaking and consuming the foods I craved. Eating excessive amounts of food gave me the control I was seeking. It also reinforced the belief that I had created about being unworthy and unattractive.

Besides my strong desire to lose the weight, my mother's role in this process is what truly allowed me to express myself and work through my emotions healthfully. My mother never judged me. My mother just loved me. She accepted me and my body for how it looked and never tried to change anything. She didn't try to control what I ate, or tell me what exercise I should have done to shed some pounds.

All she did was love me, and let me make my own decisions instead of telling me how I should be living my life. This consistent love and acceptance is what made me feel safe in confiding in her my desire to be thin.

Chapter 5

Memories of the Parents of an Overweight Child

(Jacqui)

This chapter was added after Mom and I finished writing the book. We both thought that the idea of incorporating Kim's parents' perspective of raising an overweight child was necessary to show the contrast of how a child may interpret a situation differently than what was intended by the parents.

I am writing the remainder of this chapter. I met with my grandparents at separate times without my mom present to allow them to speak freely. You may notice the stark contrast between my grandparents' recollections of my mom's childhood weight problem compared to her own account in Chapter 3 of this book.

My grandmother, Jean, explained how she grew up in the Midwest where healthy foods were not often incorporated into the daily diet of most families. She described herself as having a weight problem in grade school, but lost the excess weight before high school. Grandma attributed the weight loss to growing taller and walking to school. She also added that she has no recollection of being teased by other children or reprimanded by her parents for carrying extra poundage. Jean verbalized that she had never really had a weight problem since this period of her life.

My grandfather, Don, also grew up in the Midwest, however, he stated that he had never had a weight problem, and he was always very skinny. He was six feet tall and wrestled at 175 pounds in high school adding, "I always had a fast metabolism and I was always hyper." He also mentioned that his parents never monitored what he ate as a child.

I asked both of my grandparents about their experiences raising Mom when they saw that she was becoming overweight as a child.

I asked them if it bothered or frustrated them that Mom was overweight.

(Jean)

"Well yeah, it was frustrating, but when you have two sons and a girl, and the boys don't have any problem, then I don't know why…she would take…sneak food in her room."

(Don)

"No, it wasn't frustrating; I just didn't know how to deal with it. We knew she was overweight and we sent her to a camp in Washington state, and she came back in pretty good shape, but then she went back on the same thing, and the only thing I remember you know is I am not very good at saying 'Damn it, lose weight, or you're not going to do this or that.' But I said to her though, I said, 'Kimberly, if you get down to a decent weight, I will buy you a new car. I will buy you any car you want if you lose weight.' I wanted her to lose weight."

(Jacqui)

"I think you said once that you paid her like a dollar or some amount of money for every pound she lost."

(Jean)

"No, I never tried that kind of stuff. I think you should love them and not bribe them."

(Don)

"No, I don't think we ever did that, but I always worked so many dang hours that I kind of left everything up to Jean. It is probably my fault, if I had it to do over again, I would say, 'You gotta lose weight.' It is probably more my fault than hers (Jean).

(Jacqui)

During the interview with my grandfather, I asked him if he had any memories of Mom's weight problem being an issue between her and Grandma.

(Don)

"I don't think so, I don't think Jean ever cared if Kim was overweight. Mom and Grandma were really loving people. They take you the way you are, and so do I. When she (Kim) came back from that camp, she lost a lot of weight and we probably didn't know enough or do enough to keep her on track, and then I do know I offered, 'Kim if you lose enough weight before you graduate, I will buy you any car you want.' I remember that so succinctly and I really meant it. I said 'God I want her to be pretty, young, and slim and trim and I'm willing to do this and I really didn't have the money to do that, but I would have done it because she is my daughter and we just didn't know what to do. We tried several things and we failed. Jean and I had such a good bond about backing each other up when disciplining the kids, but with this, we just didn't know what to do."

(Jacqui)

I then switched the focus of the interview and asked my grandmother how she thought Mom perceived her weight problem.

(Jean)

"I didn't think it even bothered her, because she didn't say anything."

(Jacqui)

"Do you think that it bothered you that it didn't bother her (Kim)?"

(Jean)

"Well, yeah probably. I don't really think she thought of herself as being too heavy…she always seemed happy, and maybe she wasn't and it was just a front."

(Jacqui)

"Is there anything you would have done differently regarding Mom's weight?"

(Jean)

"It's awful hard to fix one meal for someone that is trying to lose weight, and then fix for three guys that aren't. I just felt that she would have taken smaller quantities and she never did seem to take large quantities. I don't really have any regrets, but I could have done things better I guess. I would have to have someone teach me and teach her how to not eat that much or whatever. We never ever reprimanded her for the extra weight."

(Jacqui)

As you can see, after reading the accounts from Kim, Don, and Jean, a situation experienced by all three people is remembered very differently. It is important to note that children feel deeply, and often internalize the comments and actions of their loved ones, especially their parents. Kim speaks of her feelings and how she felt shame about being overweight. Looking back, Don and Jean do not speak of feelings, but rather actions surrounding eating and exercising as being the most important approaches to handle a child's weight issue.

(Kim)

After I read this chapter, which I really wasn't supposed to be a part of, I wanted to add a few comments. It saddens me to hear my father feels that he has failed. The excess weight was not an issue that could have been successfully remedied using harsher language or stricter rules. I was using food for comfort emotionally. It has become a conditioned habit that I struggle with daily. This is not an excuse, but rather, it is the truth. It is my responsibility to address this issue as an adult. I was craving affection and more emotional bonding with my parents as a child. I believe they grew up in an era where you do not show vulnerability to your children because they believe it is a sign of weakness. I was completely consumed by this problem as a child and even today. It is shocking to me to read that both of my parents thought that it did not bother me to be so different from all the other children. I focused on things I could do successfully like studying and other activities involving my brain rather than my body, but those things are not enough to fill a craving for intimacy. Many of you may be thinking, "What? Craving for intimacy? I was lucky to even see my parents, let alone bond with them. I wasn't overweight as a result." People respond differently. Some drink, some smoke or use drugs, some people have trouble forming sustainable emotional connections with anyone as a result of this lack of intimacy with their parents. I strongly feel that parents need to be aware that when a child is very overweight, it is usually the result of an emotional issue rather than the physical consumption of food or lack of exercise. I know my parents both loved me very much as a child, but I felt my mother resented my weight problem because she felt it was a reflection of her parenting and it was easier for my father to ignore the situation rather than address the issue emotionally.

Chapter 6

Control

There are many different reasons why children gravitate to food and as a result, end up overweight. There is no one single reason for childhood obesity. You must remember every human being has a life that results from many influences and experiences. There are many children who believe that there is something very wrong with them because they are overweight and different from the other kids. This is where their self-esteem begins to erode, and food becomes the nurturer and self-soothing friend. As this unhealthy behavior continues, a negative habit is formed. We have identified three distinct behaviors that are most prevalent among overweight children. It is important to note that your child will not fit exactly into one of these groups. You may recognize that your child possesses characteristics from each category. This part of the book may be difficult to read and identify with because as parents we have tried to raise our children in the best way possible. Many of us have sworn that we would not do to our children what was done to us. Therefore, we feel we have improved upon the parenting that we received. That is probably the truth. It is a challenge to see problems both with our children and with how we have raised them, because we are so close to the situation.

There are many parents who are scared to discover the real cause of their child's problem, because that means it is a direct reflection of their parenting. While reading this chapter, try to stand back and listen to the information we have to share without getting defensive. Most of you have attempted to fix the situation multiple times unsuccessfully. It is time to broaden your perspective and consider other possibilities as the reason why your child may be overweight. The reason for this section of the book is not to direct blame or to evoke guilt to any one person or circumstance that has occurred, but rather to help you better understand why this problem may be occurring. There are many obese children from parents who also have difficulties with weight. But there are also parents who have never struggled with weight issues and cannot identify with their child or understand their behaviors with regard to food. This is an attempt to help you understand what may be occurring in your child's mind. One last comment we would like to make is that we understand you may be frustrated, angry, or even resentful of your child because you feel that you have tried everything to help them. It is okay. This is a normal reaction.

As stated above, we have observed three general types of personalities in overweight children. The first and most prevalent personality trait is the people pleaser. We know the most about this category because we both fit into this group beautifully.

These children are often assertive, polite, intelligent, and genuinely sweet children. They are easy to be around, have friends, and are obedient when dealing with authority figures. The child is more focused on other people's feelings and opinions than their own. They yearn for acceptance and positive feedback from others. This may be done as a result of living in a chaotic environment. There is often yelling or unhappiness on the part of one of the parents or both in the family. This unhappiness may be a result of a troubled marriage, blending families, sibling rivalry, addictions, or any other family problem that may result in discord in the home. The people pleaser goes through their life being selfless and giving up their happiness in an attempt to control their situation.

(Kim)

When I was about twelve years old, I would often get up early on Sunday mornings and cook an entire breakfast for my family, which included eggs, bacon, potatoes, and even homemade biscuits. I did this because I knew my mother would be happy with me. I often felt like a disappointment to her, and it felt good to be in her good graces even if only for one day.

(Jacqui)

I was most definitely a people pleaser, and tried to please everyone but was unsuccessful with my father. He was the person who I felt was judgmental of me. Hearing positive feedback as a people pleaser from other adults that I respected like my mom, my teachers, and other family members, would make me feel good. I thrived on the attention and the feelings associated with being good. I chose to avoid my father as much as possible. I used people pleasing as a tool to avoid conflict in my life.

The second personality trait or behavior of an overweight child is one who acts mean or rude to others. This child may appear defensive or unhappy. Parents need to understand these negative emotions often result from the child having been hurt or upset and does not know how to address her/his emotions in a constructive manner. These types of behaviors are also an attempt to try to control the child's environment. This is often reflective of unhappiness in the home or in their family life. As ugly as these behaviors come across, it is important to remember at the core is a person who has feelings of hurt and/or disappointment.

The third personality type is the child who rarely shows any emotion and remains quiet. This child is often labeled as shy, which may result in people assuming they are not very bright.

These children have often been those that were teased, or children and adults would make fun of their appearance. These children stay quiet in fear of being embarrassed in front of other children or family members. They choose to avoid attention and often do not get involved in extracurricular activities and isolate themselves.

A common thread in all of these personality types is that they try to anticipate what is going to happen in their lives. They want to control their environment so that nothing happens to surprise or embarrass them regarding their weight. These kids miss out on many fun activities to avoid running into an uncomfortable situation.

(Kim)

As a kid, I remember trying to avoid coed pool parties and going to the beach because I would have to wear my one piece bathing suit in front of the other kids. In high school, I was not asked to dance very often, and I also tried to avoid this embarrassing situation by staying home or being the "helpful" person who organized or ran the event. I could be busy, and not appear to be standing alone without someone asking me to dance.

People with eating disorders often try to take control of their lives using food. In the situation of an anorexic individual, the control is in restricting their intake of food to become thin. This control issue is also often a result of a feeling of loss of control in their family or home environment. These children will often feel that controlling their intake of food will help calm their emotions. They will go to great lengths to hide their behaviors, because they are chastised or reprimanded for not eating. In bulimic or binge-eaters, the control is in eating great amounts of food at one time. Sneaking food is one way they avoid the disapproving looks and judgments of other people. Compulsive overeaters also sneak food, and will often admit to eating as a way to fill up an emptiness they feel inside themselves. The food is a form of instant gratification and temporary happiness that compensates for the external turmoil in their lives. This temporary binging or constant overeating results in a self-loathing that causes more harm to the individual with regard to self-esteem and general wellbeing.

Chapter 7

Love

How many times have we all heard, "You can't love anyone else until you love yourself"? This sentence or many variations on this theme have been articulated by therapists, lifestyle gurus, and our friends and relatives who are imparting their loving wisdom upon us. This is often said when we are trying to look for or improve upon a relationship with another person. This can also ring true with our relationship to food. In order to have a healthy relationship with food, we must first love and accept ourselves. But what does this actually mean to love yourself? How exactly are we supposed to do that? As a parent, you must understand and realize this concept for yourself before you can effectively teach your child how to do the same. Loving and accepting yourself is a continuous process that some of you may have already mastered very well in your life. For those of you who have not, this may be a very beneficial learning experience for both you and your child.

First, we would like to emphatically express that children are much smarter than most people believe. Children are listening. They hear your conversations with other adults and they know how you feel regarding most subjects.

When someone we love is not behaving or performing the way we would like for them to, we often begin to get frustrated and resentful of that person. We attempt to plead, lecture, explain, and ask for things to change. When you need others to act in a different way in order for you to be happy with them, you are loving them conditionally. At this point, many of you are probably feeling defensive and wanting to justify your actions, because you believe it is for your child's own good. You may be thinking that everyone knows that when someone is overweight, they are not as healthy and usually not as happy. So of course you want them to listen to you, because their wellbeing is your main focus. That is commendable, but the best result occurs when parents also focus on their own happiness and learn to find balance in their own lives. There are many parents who will sacrifice all that they enjoy to show that they have their priorities in order. They want their child and the people around them to know that their child is at the center of their world. The problem is that these parents become tired and unhappy trying to give all of their energy and focus to someone else. They are not truly loving themselves. Your child looks to you as the center of their universe. They try to please you. You are their role model. As the old adage goes: your behaviors and actions truly do speak louder than words. Your child began studying you from the time they were born. Your children love you unconditionally.

What we do with that love determines the fate of the relationship; therefore in order for a child to value and care properly for her/himself, you must also respect and love yourself. This means taking up a hobby that you love to do, taking a weekend nap, treating yourself to a massage, or doing something that shows your child that caring for yourself is important. As her/his role model, your child will then begin to understand that s/he can love someone while properly caring for her/himself. Many people pleasers have been taught that being "selfish" is wrong. The term selfish has become very negative. Many people believe it means that you disregard the wellbeing of others and only care for yourself. We contend that the word selfish means you take care of your needs and are then able to help others in a healthy manner.

The negative comments that a child hears resonate very deeply. When an authority figure speaks negatively to a child, the child often internalizes those comments and then translates the remark to "There is something wrong with me." Often the parent or other authority figure making these types of remarks will justify their statements as jokes or harmless fun without realizing the devastating impact they have on the child's sense of self-worth.

(Kim)

I remember something that was said to me very often by people I knew and also by strangers. They would say, "You have such a pretty face." I believe these people were trying to compliment me, but all I heard was, "You have such a pretty face, if only you weren't so fat." It always hurt my feelings, but I would look at them and mutter, "Thank you" What these people were not saying is what actually what rang in my ears.

Another comment that I often heard while in fifth or sixth grade was, "You are just hanging on to your baby fat, it will all disappear once you go through puberty." This remark is just stupid (and also embarrassing for a young girl). I was overweight because I was eating the wrong foods and not exercising. I knew that, but because I was so desperate to be thin, I clung to the idea that the fat would disappear one day. When my mother told me she had been extremely overweight until seventh grade, and then it all "just came off", I remember thinking that would happen for me also. It really sounds ridiculous, but I didn't want to give up food, which had become a constant "friend" who was always there to help me feel better.

I believe my mom had become very resentful of my weight. She believes she tried "everything" that she could have done to help me lose weight. For every positive attempt she made to help me lose weight, I believe the negative comments and insults were three times more powerful.

This was my mom, my role model, I wanted her to love me more than anyone. I remember clearly, on one occasion, she was very angry about my weight. I was working at our family pharmacy, and she pulled me into a back room and told me that I looked disgusting. She went on to say, "Just look at your stomach, it looks like someone attached a shelf onto the front of you. And look at the size of your leg compared to mine, my leg is much smaller than yours." I didn't know what to say. I felt hurt and also a bit angry. I was getting tired of her belittling me. The size of her leg and mine should not have been of comparison. We were not in competition.

Five Healthy Strategies to Show Love to Your Child

1. Consistently and sincerely, tell your child "I love you."

This sounds too simple, but you would be surprised at how many children do not hear these words in a meaningful way. It is difficult for many people to say "I love you" in a sincere and genuine manner; however, anything that feels awkward or unnatural gets easier when expressed repeatedly. Let your child know your feelings. It is not weakness to show vulnerability. If you share your feelings with your child, s/he will want to fiercely protect your heart. This vulnerability shows your child that you have feelings and emotions. This behavior exemplifies being a role model, and s/he will grow up knowing that it is alright for her/his to feel a myriad of emotions.

2. Stop and listen.

When your child speaks to you, you must give them your attention. You may feel that what they have to say is not significant or relative to the topic at hand; however, it is important that your child believes what s/he has to say or feel has value. Often a child will want to tell you something, but you are in the middle of doing something else that seems like it needs to take priority. Try asking yourself at that moment if it is really more important to continue your task, or if it can be dealt with at a later time? If it cannot wait, communicate with your child that you hear them and because you want to be able to fully hear what they have to say, that you will be with them as soon as it is possible. The importance here is the respect you show your child. If your child persists in trying to talk at this point, just keep doing what you need to do, and do not give him attention until you are at a place where you are able. You have already addressed their need, and now they must learn to respect what you say.

3. Keep your child talking.

The children that you must worry about the most are those who will not express themselves. You do not always know what thoughts are running through your child's mind. It is important to acknowledge that however they are feeling is valid.

If your child makes a statement that you are unsure how to respond to, a good way to communicate that you are listening to them is to repeat what they said to you.

Example:

Child: I think it is stupid that my teacher is making us do 40 math problems tonight, it makes me so mad.

Parent: I understand it makes you angry that your teacher assigned so much homework in one evening, and I am glad that you learn so quickly.

There is no need for you to say more at this time. You may be just as angry that the teacher assigned so much work, and you may feel that too much time is being taken away from your family etc. If you have an issue with the teacher, it can be dealt directly with the teacher. The child just needs to know that you believe their feelings are important.

4. Do not make ANY negative comments about your child's weight. These children know their bodies do not look like their peers.

(Jacqui)

My mom never commented about my weight. I never felt she judged what I was eating, the quantity of what I ate, or how my body looked. My dad on the other hand, always made my extra weight a focal point. His hurtful comments resulted in my feeling that something was wrong with me that needed to be fixed. I knew if I told my mother what my dad was saying to me when she was not there, I would be punished or ridiculed even further. I even remember him saying once, "You can't go run and tell your mom this time." This made me feel angry and powerless. I felt constant unconditional love from my mom, which resulted in me approaching her when I wanted to begin losing weight.

When any adult makes your child's extra weight a focal point, the child begins to believe that this "defect" in them is part of their identity. They begin to believe they have no power when it comes to this problem. Shame and powerlessness are emotions that are so devastating to any individual. The problem is being magnified, and the child's self-confidence plummets.

5. **Focus on your child's strengths.**

It is important to verbally acknowledge what your child does well, with a sincere comment about their specific strengths or attributes.

Chapter 8

Emotional Navigation

Most people underestimate the power of the human mind. Right now, at this moment, look around and notice all of the things that have been created with the seed of a simple idea. When you truly grasp that you have the power to be, have, or do anything in this world that you desire, your world expands to another level. Your perspective broadens and allows you to realize that you control your life. Children depend on their parents, family members, teachers, and friends to guide them through their life experiences. As a parent, it is important to set boundaries for your child; however, more importantly, we need to teach our children how to interpret their thoughts and emotions. Many adults never received this instruction as they were growing up, and in turn do not know how to address the topic for themselves or for their children. As stated in previous chapters, showing your child vulnerability is important. As their role model, they will see that you can feel different emotions, and still responsibly handle situations in your life. Showing them vulnerability also establishes trust between you and your child. A child will want to approach you about their feelings. Remember, getting a child to identify how they are feeling and to speak about it is vital in creating a healthy perspective with regard to food. When a person is able to identify what they are feeling, it enables them to respond to that emotion more appropriately. If the emotion is never identified, many people numb the discomfort they are feeling with substances and/or negative behaviors throughout their lives.

For some children, disconnection from their loved ones leaves them with a feeling of emptiness, which they try to fill up with food. Food is easily accessible to them, and it is often perceived as a source of comfort and fulfillment. They begin focusing on food and connect eating with enjoyment and a false sense of happiness.

The repeated behavior becomes a habit, and is often described as a mindless action. Many adults who compulsively overeat describe this as "eating on autopilot." The person does not actually realize how much they have consumed. The child will often watch television or perform another activity while they are eating, which also becomes an unhealthy stimulus for the consumption of food. The attention is taken off of eating and onto the other pastime. When children begin eating in this unhealthy way, parents and family members become concerned and avidly focus on the child's problem. Many of these parents panic in reaction to their fear by admonishing their child for their eating behaviors. Remember, these children deeply want to please their parents, and at the same time they feel good when they eat. This often results in a clash of emotion and confusion. Perspective is the key to understanding why two people can be in the same situation, and experience completely opposite thoughts and emotions regarding the same topic. When your child conveys an emotion to you, it is critical to understand that their perspective of the situation is often magnified and different from yours. When you call your daughter/son a whale, a pig, or some other derogatory name, the child hears "I am fat and undesirable." You might be trying to send a message to the child in a less direct manner by joking or teasing with them regarding their excess weight. You feel they will "get the hint and do something to fix it." You could not be more wrong. These types of comments may cause feelings of shame for your child and they often reinforce that being overweight is part of their identity.

If someone was to make the same comment to you, as an adult, it is easier for you to disregard or brush off the comment and move on. Children tend to perseverate about the issue and play it over and over in their minds. These comments are often never forgotten and contribute to a more negative sense of self-worth from childhood and may continue throughout their adult life.

As parents and guardians, it is important to teach our children how to appropriately manage their emotions.

The following are tools to promote the conversation regarding feelings and emotions with your child.

1. **Tell your child that every feeling has a value and is important.**

   Many times we are told to ignore negative feelings, but our negative emotions serve to inform us about something that we do not like or want. It is important to communicate to your child that negative emotions help them to identify what they do want instead. Conversely, positive emotions should be verbalized and valued in the same way.

2. **Reinforce the importance of all emotions as a tool to identify desires.**

When your child feels any type of strong emotion, they need to determine *why* they are feeling it. This may be difficult if the child is very young, so you might have to ask them questions using your sense of what might be going on. Allow the child to know that you are wanting to help them figure out the situation, and that you will not be critical or upset with their answer. Do not become defensive or angry with them. They have a right to their emotions even when you do not understand them. When you are doing this, slow down and allow the child time to think and respond to your question. In this fast paced world, adults are often in such a hurry that they start offering the answers impatiently that may or may not be accurate. Remember, your child senses your emotions and feelings as they have studied you all of their lives. Often, the child will agree with your answer just to appease you.

Example:

Your seven-year-old child appears very angry, and lashes out with the following statement: "I just want to kill Ryan." The first thing you want to do is recognize your child's emotion by saying, "I understand you are very angry with Ryan, why do you feel this way?" This statement triggers your child to critically think and make a connection between their emotion and the situation at hand. Your seven-year-old may respond by saying, "Ryan called me fat and ugly." Before you begin plotting something horrible to do to Ryan, it is important to ask how your child feels about the comment. Acknowledge that it is ok to feel hurt or angry about the remark, and convey to them that we have a choice in how we react when people voice their opinions. If your child says that he feels fat and is upset about it, a healthy conversation about resolution is underway.

3. **Teach your child that the only opinion that truly matters is their view of themselves.**

This helps in creating a sense of self-reliance for the child. Do not worry that they will become selfish or uncaring. Children learn to be loving and caring in response to the behaviors they see modeled in their life by their parents and people whom they respect. This is the point where you may start asking the child what type of person they would like to be. Conversely, when your child is feeling really happy about a situation, ask them how they feel, and why they feel that way. This enables them to recognize positive emotions, and to see what they enjoy. Acknowledging other things that provide excitement and enjoyment in life lessens their fixation on food.

4. **Have your child name positive aspects of her/his life including both physical and mental attributes.**

A helpful tool is to have your child stand in front of a mirror and identify five characteristics about their body that they like. If the child is struggling to come up with an answer, you as the parent can start the process by performing the activity out loud in front of your child about yourself. If your child still cannot name positive body attributes about her/himself, ask them what other aspects they enjoy about their life. You may choose to have your child write in a journal daily about something for which they are grateful. Although the goal is to have the child accept and love their body as it is, just the process of listing grateful characteristics reduces negativity, and offers a more positive perspective regarding the child's view of her/his life. Do not overdo it on the praise. Children are smart and realize when you are overly emphasizing a point.

(Kim):

I was elated the first time I ever remembered something positive being said about me from my mother. My mom, my two brothers, and I were sitting at the kitchen table. My mom said, "Of all of you children, I believe that Kim has the best head on her shoulders. I think in an emergency she would know what to do." I initially felt badly for my brothers, because I was usually the one on the other end of these comments. Nevertheless, I heard "Kim is responsible." I took this comment to heart, and continued to be very responsible throughout my life. I believed my mother's comment just because I heard her say it.

That is the power of parenting. Children are extremely impressionable, especially when their parents speak about them. You can use this information in a positive way to help your child feel better about her/himself and to improve poor self-esteem. If your child overhears you making a positive comment regarding one of her/his talents, s/he will usually go to great lengths to keep demonstrating that ability.

It is important that you do not make this obvious by exaggerating. Remember, your child will pick up on your insincerity if comments are taken overboard. If you are speaking with another adult, make sure this person is also aware of what you are doing, so that they do not counter the compliment with negativity.

Chapter 9

Everyone Can Learn to Love Exercise

(Jacqui)

"No one hated exercise more than I did as a child. Just the thought of going to physical education class used to make my stomach churn. I never verbalized my hatred for PE class, but tried to manipulate my way out of it many times. I was overweight and was rarely teased by anyone about my excess weight, but I was very self-conscious about it. I would even go into the bathroom stall and lock the door to change my clothes, while all of the other girls changed in the open room. Because of my excess weight, it took more effort to move and I was very uncomfortable. When we played flag football, I would run to the belt bag before anyone else. I had to find a solid white belt because they were the only ones I knew would fit around my waist. The panic to make it to the bag and grab the right belt was intense. I knew if the belt didn't fit, that

I would be humiliated and that thought was petrifying. It is amazing to look back at the feelings that I had towards exercise as a child and how I have transformed my attitude about exercise into such a positive experience. It now plays such a central role and is a priority in my life."

If you really love exercise it does not seem like a chore; it is something you love and want to do. Of course, there will be days when the thought of exercise is not appealing and staying home on the couch would be much more convenient; however, remembering the good feelings of moving your body after exercise will propel you to take action.

Many parents tend to convey to their children that exercise is a painful and difficult experience that is necessary to achieve weight loss. How many times have you heard "No pain, no gain!"? Exercise needs to be viewed as desirable rather than as a chore or punishment for excess weight. A parent's positive perspective regarding exercise can be a powerful motivating force for their children. If children associate negative feelings around exercise at a young age, they carry those same feelings into adulthood. The goal of exercising is to maintain a healthy mind and body. This is very therapeutic in that a person is caring for her/himself, which enhances a sense of self-importance. For many people, including children, exercise can provide an outlet to release stress and anxiety in a positive manner.

(Jacqui)

"I can still remember the night that I approached my mom about losing weight. I knew that exercise should probably be a part of my lifestyle, but I still wasn't happy about it. The only experiences that I had regarding exercise up to this point in my life were very negative. My mom bought a treadmill for our family to help me in achieving my goal. My father had left our family and I was relieved. He had been the one pressuring me to lose weight and to

exercise. Once his forceful, demanding presence was gone, I was able to move forward and do something positive for myself. When I began exercising, it was a chore and it seemed boring to me. I knew that exercise needed to be a part of achieving my goal. I really liked music, so I decided to listen to music while I exercised. I would get myself entrenched in the lyrics and I was able to release my anger while I ran on the treadmill. I even had episodes where I cried while I was running. The feeling of letting go that came after I finished exercising each time felt so good to me. It gave me a sense of power. This can be invigorating especially to people who have been victims of verbal or physical abuse of any kind. There is a feeling of powerlessness for people who have been abused that is often difficult to overcome. Exercise played a large role in helping me regain my sense of power."

(Kim)

"As I just read the quote above from Jacqui, as an overweight parent with a sedentary lifestyle, I realize I did not promote exercise or health as much as I should have. As parents, we should always be looking to help our children have a better life experience. As adults, we need to continue to learn to grow. Although I had my children involved in soccer, swimming, dance, etc., I was not living the lifestyle of health and fitness or experiencing the benefits that come from living healthfully. I was not a good role model for my children in this capacity."

The type of exercise that is chosen is irrelevant. Parents should not dictate what type of exercise their kids engage in, or force them to participate in a certain sport. You may be thinking, "Well, that counts out any sport that takes physical exertion with my child. He will probably choose to play chess or enter a yo-yo tournament." Hold on, it is not that dismal. Remember, some kids just do not feel like they fit in with others, or they remember the horror of being one of the last kids chosen for the team in PE class. Once again, avoiding exercise helps them to feel safe and allows them to escape potential judgement or ridicule.

(Kim)

"As a small child, I really enjoyed dancing, and my parents put me in a dance class. I did this for several years, but as I gained weight, I was very worried about having to wear a leotard in front of other children. I never shared how I felt with any of my friends as I was so embarrassed that I was different. Some of my friends became very involved in ballet and went on to become quite talented in ballet, but my fear was so great of being teased that I stopped dancing all together. I never told my parents how I felt because I felt ashamed of my body. At the same time, I also did not want to swim anymore, because I could not wear a two-piece bathing suit like all of my friends. This pattern became very

prevalent in my life, and I began staying inside the house and leading a sedentary lifestyle. I would watch television and wander in and out of the kitchen learning to eat snacks and high-calorie foods when no one else was home. I would avoid being judged at all costs. This was when food became my friend."

People who are extremely overweight often become mentally dissociated from their bodies. They stop moving or acknowledging the mind-body connection. Often, exercise feels so difficult for an overweight person of any age, and they become consumed in negative feelings during exercise. They want to avoid this discomfort at all costs. Kids will remember good feelings associated with exercise also, and it will motivate them to keep moving their bodies. This is why as a parent, your role is to show your children how to associate positive feelings with exercise. Associating these new aspects with movement plants a seed in your child's mind for a healthy and active lifestyle in the future.

This can be accomplished most easily through communication between you and your child.

The following are suggestions regarding ways you can communicate with your child about developing a positive perspective towards exercise:

1. **Ask your child if there is a sport they are interested in playing.**

   If they do not verbalize any interest, ask them what they would like to do to help move their body in a healthy way. This may include playing tag or hide-n-seek. It is ok, as long as they understand that they need to care for their body in a positive manner.

2. **For those parents who do not live a very active lifestyle, ask your child to help you become healthier.**

Express your desire to be healthy. Remember, it is important to your child to spend time with you. They love you and want to please you. It will make them happy and proud to be able to help you accomplish your goals also. You may want to begin walking with them. If you have babies or younger children, load everyone up in strollers and have your children see that exercise is a normal part of daily life.

3. **If you notice that your child seems interested in watching a sport other kids are playing, or on television, ask her/him if s/he might want to join a team and try it out to see if they like it.**

At this point, you may make a deal with your child to try the sport for a certain period. This allows the child enough time to get through the difficult skill-building process and decide if they enjoy the sport or not. After the child has engaged in the sport for the period of time agreed upon, do not be a parent who presses the child to continue the sport if they genuinely verbalize that they want to quit. The purpose of joining the sport or team is to develop a type of exercise the child enjoys.

4. **Mention how good your body feels after engaging in physical activity.**

This tool aids the parent in communicating their own positive feelings regarding exercise to their child. Express to her/him how much more energy you have, how much happier you feel, and how much more alive you feel after you exercise. Talk about the positive feelings regarding exercise in a colorful way to enhance the imagery of the activity in your child's mind. For example, you may talk about the increased oxygen in your brain, which causes your thoughts to be clearer. You can mention the wonderful feeling of your lungs expanding as your breathing gets heavier. It is a pleasurable feeling when you experience a rush of endorphins throughout your body. Explain to her/him that exercising stimulates a sense of accomplishment that is felt when one pushes her/his body beyond its comfort zone.

5. **If you are unable to walk or exercise, try stretching movements.**

This can be accomplished in your own living room. Play music they enjoy. Laugh, dance, and make it fun while you move. This can be a special time that you share with your child.

After the exercise is over, make sure to make a positive comment about your child's performance. The type, duration, and skill level are irrelevant. This is not the time to criticize agility or talent. If your child expresses joy and interest in the particular activity s/he has participated in, remind them of the positive feelings they have while engaging in this activity. If your child points out her/his mistakes, redirect the conversation by commenting on something they did well. Remind her/him that it takes time to develop skills and if you are able, you might offer to get them some additional coaching if interest is present. Remember, this is about connecting positive feelings with a healthy lifestyle.

Chapter 10

Don't Underestimate the Power of a Healthy Mind

(Kim)

In my psychiatric practice, both a parent and a child will come into my office. Often parents will tell me that there is something wrong with the child's behavior and that s/he is causing upheaval in the family or at school. After a brief discussion, I will ask the parent to leave the room and speak with the child alone. Most often, as soon as the parent leaves and I begin speaking with the child, s/he will open up and talk about issues they will not divulge to their parent. As a parent, this should not offend you, because most often your child is afraid of upsetting or disappointing you. They believe they are protecting you. They love you so much, but do not know how to adequately express their feelings. Most of the time, the child will begin to cry and the emotions pour out. For example, they may tell me, "Mom has a new boyfriend and she is with him all the time," or, "Dad works all the time and gets mad at me a lot." Sometimes the child will admit to acting up because they want attention from their parent. Children study the behavior of adults, especially those they love and hold dear. Children watch their parents react to all type of situations. Because children want to please their parents, they will respond using behaviors that they think the parent will approve of. It is at this moment when they need to be asked what feelings they are experiencing. When the child responds, proceed by assuring her/him that their emotions are relevant whether you feel they expressed those feelings in an appropriate manner or not. These feelings for the child are often magnified and they do not know how to express them in a healthy way. If the child does not feel that you are acknowledging their feelings, they may learn to keep quiet and will not share their feelings outwardly.

This chapter of our book concentrates on the creation of a healthy mind with respect to food. Children focus more of their attention on the flavor and quantity of what they are eating rather than on the quality of the food they consume. When the concentration on food becomes obsessive, it is usually a manifestation of the suppression of fear. When the volume of food consumed is excessive, it is often a sign of the child trying to "fill-up" an emotional void in her/his life. As a parent, you may be wondering how on earth your child could have an emotional void. At this point, refer back to Chapter 2 about trauma. What you may view as a natural part of living may be experienced very differently to another human being. As parents and guardians, we must redirect the focus from food to a new goal of a healthy mind and body. This will empower the child to learn how to make choices that result in a desired goal. This new process has the potential to impact other areas of the child's life. With each successful accomplishment, a person becomes more confident in her/his ability to achieve other aspirations. This is the mechanism for building self-esteem. The individual begins to believe in her/himself and find a greater sense of self-worth. Parents who have never used food for comfort may have trouble understanding how food and self-worth are related. We would urge that individual to embrace a new perspective. Excessive focus on the consumption of food is the same avoidance mechanism demonstrated by people who abuse all types of substances such as alcohol or drugs. This is a form of addiction. The word addiction is powerful, and most people do not want to associate themselves with this term. Addiction is a habit born from fear. Addiction can be overcome.

The balance of this chapter is geared toward providing parents with tools to redirect the mental focus from food to other more healthy external stimuli.

Helpful Tools:

1. **Speak with your child as if they are intelligent.**

   Do not talk down to them. Parents and other adults often treat children using "baby" language. Children are smarter than most adults realize. They can understand the concepts that are being addressed in this book. You may have to give examples to further illustrate the ideas, but do not underestimate your child's ability to comprehend issues.

2. **Concentrate on healthy eating, not calorie or macronutrient counting.**

   We want to create a mental picture for the child of how a healthy body looks and feels. Many parents may believe that teaching their child how to count calories may be beneficial; however, this begins the process of dieting and obsessing over numbers. If your child tells you that they do not know what a healthy body looks and feels like, start the process by explaining your perspective of a healthy body. For example, you may comment on the feeling of being light, happy, and full of energy.

3. **Communicate to your child that s/he has the power to create her/his future.**

We have both witnessed many parents saying things to their children such as, "This food will make you fat." Food does not have the power to make anyone fat, and when you make these statements, a false premise is being reinforced. How often do you hear people making reference to not having the ability to control what foods they consume? "I saw this piece of cake and had to have it, I just can't say no." The focus has been taken off the desired goal, and has left the person powerless in a situation they want to change.

Simple language often is a mirror of your true thoughts and beliefs, and should be chosen carefully.

4. **Do not single out the overweight child's "problem" or allow a situation where s/he feels self-conscious, if possible.**

If you are a parent who is overweight and/or is not eating healthfully, take this opportunity to develop a new lifestyle along with your child. It is difficult to go to a fast food restaurant and order junk food for everyone else, while telling your overweight child that s/he needs to order a salad to lose the excess weight. We understand that everyone is busy, and this process of developing a healthy lifestyle is not convenient; however, you must understand this is a priority that will become a habit over time. If a child goes to a birthday party, allow them to participate fully in the party activities including eating the birthday cake, etc. After the party, when you have a minute alone, ask her/him if they feel uncomfortable due to the sugar overload. You may want to also verbalize your personal discomfort after excess sugar consumption. If s/he responds to your question with a "no" that is fine. The crucial element here is focusing on the child's feelings and the physical cues triggered by the body.

5. **Help your child to understand the composition of foods and how they are utilized in the body.**

Explain how protein helps to build muscles, and identify foods that are protein-rich. This tool is especially effective for children who are very active or enjoy sports. For example, fruits help in cellular recovery, provide energy, and are a good source of fiber. Explain to your child how fruits may help them to run faster or enhance the performance of a certain activity. For those parents who are not savvy about this topic, take this opportunity to educate yourself about the composition and function of healthy foods. Learn how to read food labels, and how to avoid ingredients that make people feel poorly. You may share this information with your child, and depending upon their age, you may be able to do this together. The goal is to communicate the benefits of healthy eating and that the responsibility of making healthy food choices eventually will lie upon the child. Remember, the focus is being shifted from food being "bad" to food being a source of energy and fuel for the body. Teach the child to listen to the signals the body gives that it needs nourishment.

6. **Never call your child a name that involves excess weight, even in a teasing manner.**

7. **Praise your child when they are making progress.**

Prompt your child to express the positive feelings they are experiencing when they are doing something healthy for their body. Share your feelings with your child; remember, vulnerability is a positive emotion to share with them.

8. **Find an outlet for your child to express her/his feelings and to release anxiety.**

We live in a fast-paced society and often ignore our feelings. If you have the resources to get your child into a therapist, it may be beneficial. Teaching a child meditation, biofeedback, yoga, and other relaxation techniques will allow them to self-soothe in a more healthy fashion. You can go online and find guided meditations from universities and other sites that do not cost money and are easy to utilize. This can also be a family event. Exercise is a natural way to release anxiety. Family walks, bicycle rides, etc. are healthy habits that often make the family unit stronger. Remember, your child wants to spend time with you and to be close to you.

9. **If your child eats something fattening or takes second helpings at a meal, do not convey disapproval to her/him either verbally or through your body language.** Your child will be looking for your reaction. It is better to not react at all. When your child chooses to have a second helping, it may trigger an uncomfortable bodily reaction. For example, if s/he chooses to have a second helping of lasagna, it may hurt their stomach after consumption or

give them a feeling a being too full. This is an opportunity to lovingly verbalize the connection between the excess food consumed and the feelings of discomfort that the child is experiencing. Remember, a child will respond to love and acceptance eagerly. You want them to know you love them unconditionally. If you are constantly upset over your child's weight, look more deeply within yourself to see why this is such an emotionally-charged subject for YOU. Usually there are unresolved issues that need to be addressed.

Conclusion

This book has covered a great amount of material. Of all the tools mentioned to help your child when struggling with a weight issue, the most important aspect to be addressed is that of love. We know you love your child, and that is why utilizing these tools in a consistent manner will result in abundant rewards. When we look back to the things in life that are the most important as a child, feelings are at the forefront. Often the feelings that stem from the relationship between children and their parents or other influential individuals are the most reflected upon by the child. The feelings and the relationships create the belief system that the child usually uses throughout their life. The goal of this book is to create a healthy mental foundation with regard to food. If the feelings of accountability, being a good person, and self-love are instilled into our children, they will be able to trust themselves. They will value who they are, and be ready to make more sound decisions for their lives. People act upon their belief systems. These beliefs are created from what we are told, what we observe, and also from decades of behaviors that become who we are. If the premise of the belief system is faulty, the behaviors that result will reflect the negative or injurious thoughts that have been developed. For some children who have experienced abuse of any kind, the act of over-eating is a form of self-abuse that feels familiar. If the belief is "I am good," then the person will treat her/himself with more respect. Many people have endured years or even decades of negative reinforcement involving food such as: eating for comfort, boredom, or as a reaction to stressful situations. These habits have often become conditioned and feel automatic. This is a far more difficult challenge to overcome, and requires a more extensive set of tools to tackle. The identification and application of these types of tools will be discussed in a future book. Children do not have those years of negative reinforcement. If they are given positive attention and a healthy foundation with regard to food, exercise, and feelings, they are able to reverse the destructive habits more quickly. The new positive lifestyle that is formed will become automatic and will feel normal to the child. Professional therapy is often a valuable aid for individuals of any age. Some children may need this type of help to overcome their interpretation of life situations. You are the most important role model and influence in your child's life. Now is the time for action...your child can't weight.